GLOBAL REFLECTIONS.

A Journal for Self Discovery

Welcome to your travel journal!

Travel is about so much more than just visiting new places. It's about growth, adventure, exploration, freedom, escapism, learning, and facing fears. It's about expanding our horizons and challenging our biases. It's about discovering new cultures, people, and ways of life.

This journal is a powerful tool for capturing and reflecting on these experiences. It allows us to document our adventures, process our emotions, and make meaningful connections with the world around us. Writing in a travel journal can also provide a sense of clarity and perspective, helping us to identify patterns and challenges and make positive changes in our lives.

In this journal, you will have the opportunity to explore your own growth and learning through a variety of writing prompts and inspiring quotes. By reflecting on your experiences, goals, and challenges, you can gain a greater understanding of yourself and the ways in which you can nurture your own personal and professional growth. It also includes a bucket list checklist for you to mark off all the amazing places you've been and things you've accomplished.

Plus, there are blank pages for you to write about specific travel experiences, including the date, location, who attended, your rating of the experience, the best part, and what you learned.

We hope that this journal will be a source of inspiration and support as you embark on your journey of exploration and growth through travel.

Have a great journey,
Patricia Keller

"The world is a book and those who do not travel read only one page." - Augustine of Hippo

Reflect on your travel experiences so far and think about what you have learned from them. How have they changed you or helped you grow as a person?

"The biggest risk is not taking any risk. In a world that is changing quickly, the only strategy that is guaranteed to fail is not taking risks." - Mark Zuckerberg

Write about a time when you took a risk while traveling, and how it paid off or didn't go as planned. What did you learn from the experience?

THE WORLD IS
A BOOK, AND
THOSE WHO DO
NOT TRAVEL
READ ONLY
ONE PAGE.

"I believe that women have a unique role to play in the world, and I believe that women have the power to change the world." - Angela Davis

Write about a time when your travels helped you to feel more empowered or inspired to make a positive impact in the world. What did you learn from the experience?

"The beauty of the world lies in the diversity of its people." - Unknown

Reflect on the ways in which your travels have helped you to gain a new understanding of different lifestyles and ways of living.

"Travel and change of place impart new vigor to the mind." - Seneca

Consider your passions and goals. What do you want to achieve or experience in your life, and how can travel help you get there?

"Travel is the only thing you buy that makes you richer." - Anonymous

Reflect on your personal growth while traveling. What have you learned about yourself and your capabilities, and how have these lessons impacted your life?

THE JOURNEY
NOT THE ARRIVAL
MATTERS.

"Don't listen to what they say. Go see." - Unknown

Write about a place you visited that surprised you in some way or challenged your preconceived notions. What did you learn from the experience?

"Travel is my therapy." -Unknown

Write about a fun activity or adventure you experienced while traveling and how it impacted your life.

"Man cannot discover new oceans unless he has the courage to lose sight of the shore." – Andre Gide

What is the most courageous thing you have ever done? How did it make you feel? List 3 ways you can be more courageous in your daily life.

"Travel is an investment in yourself." -Unknown

Write about a memorable experience you had while traveling and how it has influenced your future plans or goals. What are you looking forward to experiencing or achieving as a result of this experience? How has this experience helped you to grow and discover more about yourself?

TRAVEL IS FATAL TO PREJUDICE, BIGOTRY, AND NARROW-MINDEDNESS.

"The world is a canvas for your imagination." - Henry David Thoreau

Write about a place you have visited that has left a lasting impression on you. Why was it meaningful to you and what did you learn from the experience?

"The journey not the arrival matters." - T.S. Eliot

Consider the values that are important to you, and how they have been reflected or challenged in your travel experiences.

"Travel is fatal to prejudice, bigotry, and narrow-mindedness." - Mark Twain

Write about a time when your travels exposed you to new cultures or ways of thinking that challenged your beliefs. How did this impact you?

"The world is a beautiful place and worth fighting for." - Ernest Hemingway

Write about a place you have visited that has inspired you to take action or make a positive impact in some way. How did the experience inspire you?

THE REAL VOYAGE
OF DISCOVERY
CONSISTS
NOT IN SEEKING
NEW LANDSCAPES,
BUT IN HAVING
NEW EYES.

"Traveling is a brutality. It forces you to trust strangers and to lose sight of all that familiar comfort of home and friends."

- Cheryl Strayed

Write about a time when you had to rely on the kindness of strangers while traveling. How did the experience impact you?

"Because in the end, you won't remember the time you spent working in the office or moving your lawn. Climb that goddamn mountain."- Jack Kerouac

Write about a time when travel helped you feel more alive or helped you to see life in a new way. What did you learn from the experience?

"The use of traveling is to regulate imagination by reality, and instead of thinking how things may be, to see them as they are." - Samuel Johnson

Write about a time when your travels helped you to see things more clearly or in a different way. What did you learn from the experience?

"The more I wander, the more I realize how much I love my home." - Unknown

Write about a time when your travels made you appreciate your home or your loved ones in a new way. What did you learn from the experience?

WE TRAVEL, INITIALLY, TO LOSE OURSELVES; AND WE TRAVEL, NEXT, TO FIND OURSELVES. WE TRAVEL TO OPEN OUR HEARTS AND EYES AND LEARN MORE ABOUT THE WORLD.

"The world is a stage and we are all players." - William Shakespeare

Write about a time when you felt like you were part of something bigger while traveling. What was the experience like and what did you learn from it?

"Life is a journey, not a destination." - Ralph Waldo Emerson

Write about a time when the journey itself was more meaningful than the destination. What made it special to you?

"The best journeys in life are those that answer questions you never thought to ask." - Rich Ridgeway

Write about a time when your travels helped you to discover something new about yourself or the world. What did you learn from the experience?

"One's destination is never a place, but a new way of seeing things." - Henry Miller

Write about a place you have visited that has helped you see things in a new way or opened your eyes to something new. What did you learn from the experience?

I HAVEN'T BEEN EVERYWHERE, BUT IT'S ON MY LIST.

"I met a lot of people in Europe, I even encountered myself."

\- James Baldwin

Write about a time when your travels helped you to better understand yourself or your own identity. What did you learn from the experience?

"The journey of a thousand miles begins with a single step."

- Lao Tzu

Write about the first time you traveled alone or to a new place. What was the experience like and what did you learn from it?

"I would rather own a little and see the world than own the world and see a little of it." - Alexander Sattler

Write about a time when you sacrificed material possessions or comfort for the sake of travel and the experience you gained from it. What did you learn from the experience?

"The only true limitation is the one you set for yourself." - Oprah Winfrey

Write about a time when you pushed yourself out of your comfort zone while traveling and what you learned from the experience.

LIFE IS EITHER
A DARING
ADVENTURE OR
NOTHING
AT ALL.

"The world is round and the place which may seem like the end may also be only the beginning." - Ivy Baker Priest

Write about a time when you reached the end of a journey and realized it was just the beginning of something new. What did you learn from the experience?

"There is no greater education than one that is self-driven." - Neil deGrasse Tyson

Write about a time when you took the initiative to plan and execute a solo trip. What did you learn from the experience?

"The world is a small place, and we are all connected." - Maya Angelou

Write about a time when your travels helped you to feel more connected to the world or to others. What did you learn from the experience?

"To travel is to discover that everyone is wrong about other countries." - Aldous Huxley

Write about a time when your travels challenged your preconceived notions or stereotypes about a particular place or group of people. What did you learn from the experience?

TO TRAVEL IS
TO DISCOVER
THAT EVERYONE
IS WRONG
ABOUT OTHER
COUNTRIES.

"The goal is to die with memories not dreams." - Unknown

Write about a time when you felt like you were part of something bigger while traveling. What was the experience like and what did you learn from it?

"Each new destination is am opportunity to learn and grow, and the more you explore, the more confident you become in your ability to navigate new situations and challenges." – Mytravelcrush

Write about a time when your travels helped you to feel more confident in yourself or your own abilities. What did you learn from the experience?

"I am a woman, phenomenally. Phenomenal woman, that's me." - Maya Angelou

Write about a time when you felt proud of your identity or your own strength while traveling. What did the experience mean to you?

"The only way for a woman, as for a man, to find herself, to know herself as a person, is by creative work of her own." - Betty Friedan

Write about a creative project or pursuit you undertook while traveling and what you learned from it.

TRAVEL IS MORE
THAN THE
SEEING OF
SIGHTS; IT IS A
CHANGE THAT
GOES ON, DEEP
AND PERMANENT,
IN THE IDEAS OF
LIVING.

"I am not afraid to speak up for what I believe in." - Alice Walker

Write about a time when your travels inspired you to speak up or take action for a cause you believe in. What did you learn from the experience?

"True friends never apart maybe in distance never in heart."
– Helen Keller

Reflect on how the love and support of others has shaped your own growth and development. Write how you work to cultivate a positive and nurturing environment for yourself and those around you.

"It's not about the destination, it's about the journey. And the journey of self-discovery is ongoing." - Unknown

Write about a time when your travels helped you to better understand yourself or your own values. What did you learn from the experience?

"The greatest discovery of all time is that a person can change his future by merely changing his attitude." - Oprah Winfrey

Write about a time when you had a shift in perspective while traveling and how it impacted your journey. What did you learn from the experience?

I MET A LOT
OF PEOPLE IN
EUROPE, I EVEN
ENCOUNTERED
MYSELF.

"The only way to do great work is to love what you do." - Steve Jobs

Write about a time when you found your passion or purpose while traveling. What did the experience mean to you?

"To be yourself in a world that is constantly trying to make you something else is the greatest accomplishment." - Ralph Waldo Emerson

Write about a time when your travels helped you to feel more comfortable in your own skin or more confident in your own identity. What did you learn from the experience?

"Happiness is not something ready made. It comes from your own actions." - Dalai Lama

Write about a time when your travels brought you joy or happiness, and what you did to contribute to that feeling.

"The mind is everything; what you think, you become." - Buddha

Write about a time when your thoughts or mindset had a significant impact on your travel experience. What did you learn from the experience?

THE BIGGEST
ADVENTURE
YOU CAN TAKE IS
TO LIVE THE
LIFE OF YOUR
DREAMS.

"The world is my country, all mankind are my brethren, and to do good is my religion." - Unknown

Write about a time when your travels helped you to feel more connected to humanity or inspired you to do good in the world. What did you learn from the experience?

"The journey toward self-discovery begins with a single step, and that step is often taking a moment to pause and reflect." - Unknown

Write about a time when you took the time to slow down and reflect while traveling. What did you learn from the experience?

"The best way to find yourself is to lose yourself in the service of others." - Mahatma Gandhi

Write about a time when your travels led you to volunteer or serve others, and what you learned from the experience.

"Traveling leaves you speechless, then turns you into a storyteller." - Ibn Battuta

Write about a memorable travel experience and how it has inspired you to share your story with others.

DARE TO
LIVE THE LIFE
YOU ALWAYS
WANTED.

"To travel is to live." - Hans Christian Andersen

Reflect on the different ways in which travel has enriched your life. What have you gained from your experiences and how have they impacted your perspective on the world?

"Travel brings power and love back into your life." –Rumi

How have your travels impacted your relationship with your family, friends, and how have you navigated any challenges or differences in perspective? What were some of the strategies you used to cope with their objections or concerns, and how did these experiences help you to become more resilient and self-reliant?

"The real voyage of discovery consists not in seeking new landscapes, but in having new eyes." - Marcel Proust

Write about a time when your travels helped you to see the world in a new way or changed your perspective.

"Traveling is like flirting with life. It's like saying, 'I would stay and love you, but I have to go; this is my station.'" - Lisa St. Aubin de Terán

Reflect on the relationships you have formed while traveling. How have they impacted your life and how have you changed as a result of them?

LIFE IS A JOURNEY, NOT A DESTINATION.

"The best journeys in life are those that answer questions you never thought to ask." - Rich Ridgeway

Write about a travel experience that led you to discover something new about yourself or the world.

"Travel has a way of shaking up the soul and clearing the mind." - Unknown

Write about a time when traveling helped you to improve your mental health or find clarity in a difficult situation.

"Friendship is born at that moment when one person says to another, 'What! You too? I thought I was the only one.'" - C.S. Lewis

Reflect on the friendships you have formed while traveling and how they have enriched your life.

"Traveling is like taking a shower. It washes away the stress and rejuvenates the spirit." - Unknown

Write about a time when traveling helped you to reduce stress or find relaxation. How did it impact your well-being?

A JOURNEY
OF A THOUSAND
MILES BEGINS
WITH A SINGLE
STEP.

"I am an example of what is possible when girls from the very beginning of their lives are loved and nurtured by people around them. I was surrounded by extraordinary women in my life who taught me about quiet strength and dignity." - Michelle Obama

Write about the influential women in your life, including those you have met while traveling, and how they have impacted your journey. What have you learned from them?

"The greatest adventure is what lies ahead. Today and tomorrow are yet to be said. The chances, the changes are all yours to make. The mold of your life is in your hands to break." - J.R.R. Tolkien

Reflect on your future travel goals and how they align with your personal and professional aspirations.

"Travel allows us to rediscover the beauty in the world and ourselves." - Unknown

Write about a time when traveling helped you to find beauty and appreciation in the world around you. How did it change your perspective?

"Life is a journey, and the journey itself is home." - Matsuo Bashō

Reflect on the concept of "home" and how your travels have influenced your understanding of it.

COLLECT
MOMENTS,
NOT THINGS.

"Travel and change of place impart new vigor to the mind." - Seneca

Write about a time when traveling helped you to feel energized and motivated. What sparked this feeling for you?

"If you look at what you have in life, you'll always have more. If you look at what you don't have in life, you'll never have enough." – Oprah

Reflect on the ways in which traveling has expanded your understanding of the world and its diverse cultures.

"Adventure may hurt you but monotony will kill you." - Unknown

Write about a time when traveling helped you to break out of a monotonous routine and try something new.

"One's destination is never a place, but a new way of seeing things." - Henry Miller

Reflect on the ways in which traveling has helped you to see the world and yourself in a new light.

NOT ALL CLASSROOMS HAVE FOUR WALLS.

"Traveling is like a mirror that reflects back to us who we are and what we believe in." - Unknown

Reflect on the ways in which your travels have helped you to gain a deeper understanding of yourself and your beliefs.

"Traveling has taught me that the world is so much bigger than my own little bubble, and it's given me a new perspective on life." - Unknown

Write about a time when your travels helped you to gain a new perspective on the world and its complexities.

"Travel forces you to confront your own privilege and the ways in which it shapes your perception of the world." - Unknown

Reflect on the ways in which your travels have helped you to better understand issues of race, class, gender and privilege.

"Traveling helps us to see the world through a different lens, and to understand the complexity of society and social structures in different cultures." - Unknown

Write about a time when your travels helped you to gain a deeper understanding of the societal and cultural differences in the places you visited.

THE BEST
JOURNEYS
IN LIFE ARE
THOSE THAT
ANSWER
QUESTIONS YOU
NEVER THOUGHT
TO ASK.

"Traveling helps to break down the gender roles and expectations that we may have been conditioned to follow."
- Unknown

Reflect on the ways in which your travels have helped you to gain a new understanding of gender roles and expectations in different cultures.

"Traveling forces us to confront the ways in which capitalism shapes the world and the way we live our lives." - Unknown

Write about a time when your travels helped you to gain a deeper understanding of capitalism and its impact on society.

"Traveling can be challenging, but it's through facing these difficulties that we grow and learn about ourselves." - Unknown

Reflect on the growth you have experienced while traveling and how you have benefited in all areas of your life.

"Loneliness is a common feeling when traveling, but it's through these moments of solitude that we can truly connect with ourselves and the world around us." - Unknown

Write about a time when you felt lonely while traveling and how you coped with the feeling. What lessons did you learn?

TO MY MIND, THE GREATEST REWARD AND LUXURY OF TRAVEL IS TO BE ABLE TO EXPERIENCE EVERYDAY THINGS AS IF FOR THE FIRST TIME, TO BE IN A POSITION IN WHICH ALMOST NOTHING IS SO FAMILIAR IT IS TAKEN FOR GRANTED.

"Homesickness is a natural part of the traveling experience, but it's also an opportunity to appreciate the people and things we have in our lives." - Unknown

Reflect on times when you have experienced homesickness while traveling and how you have coped with the feeling.

"Traveling as a woman, minority, or solo traveler can bring its own set of challenges, but it's also an opportunity to challenge societal expectations and stereotypes." - Unknown

Write about a time when you faced specific challenges while traveling as a woman, minority, or solo traveler, and how you overcame them.

"Traveling can be intimidating, but it's through facing our fears and stepping out of our comfort zones that we grow and learn the most." - Unknown

Reflect on a time when you faced a fear while traveling and how you overcame it. What did you learn from the experience?

"Traveling alone can be a liberating and empowering experience, but it's also important to take precautions and be aware of potential dangers." - Unknown

Write about a time when you traveled alone and the precautions you took to ensure your safety. How did the experience impact you?

ALL YOU'VE GOT TO DO IS DECIDE TO GO AND THE HARDEST PART IS OVER.

"Some beautiful paths can't be discovered without getting lost."

Reflect on the challenges you have faced while traveling and how you overcame them. What did you learn about yourself in the process?

"People don't take trips, trips take people." – John Steinbeck

Write about a place you have visited that has left a lasting impression on you. Why was it meaningful to you and what did you learn from the experience?

"Travel isn't always pretty. It isn't always comfortable. Sometimes it hurts, it even breaks your heart. But that's okay. The journey changes you; it should change you. It leaves marks on your memory, on your consciousness, on your heart, and on your body. You take something with you. Hopefully, you leave something good behind." – Anthony Bourdain

Write about a time when traveling was uncomfortable and how it impacted you or changed your thinking about travel.

"Travel is never a matter of money but of courage." – Paolo Coelho

List the fears or doubts holding you back from pursuing the life you want. What are your dreams and goals for your life? How can you use what you have learned from your travels to continue learning and growing as a person?

WHEREVER YOU GO BECOMES A PART OF YOU SOMEHOW.

"Although it can be difficult to deal with family members who don't support my travels, I have learned to value my own passions and goals and to advocate for myself." – Unknown

How have you had to assert your own values and goals in the face of family members who don't support your desire to travel? What were some of the most difficult or frustrating situations you faced, and how did you learn to value and advocate for yourself in these situations?

"Food is our common ground, a universal experience." - James Beard

What were some of the unique or memorable foods that you encountered during your travels? How did they differ from what you are used to, and what did you learn about the culture and traditions behind them?

What are your upcoming travels plans? What do you hope to gain, experience or learn?

TRAVEL - THE BEST
WAY TO BE LOST
AND FOUND
AT THE SAME
TIME.

TRAVEL DIARY

Date: ______________________________

Location: ___________________________

Rate experience:

____

Write about your experiences. What was the best part of your experience? Who were you traveling with you or were you solo? How did the trip impact you? What did you learn? What if any challenges?

____

____

____

____

____

____

____

____

____

____

____

____

____

Date: ______________________________

Location:______________________________

Rate experience:

____

Write about your experiences. What was the best part of your experience? Who were you traveling with you or were you solo? How did the trip impact you? What did you learn? What if any challenges?

____

____

____

____

____

____

____

____

____

____

____

____

____

____

____

Date: ______________________________

Location:____________________________

Rate experience:

____

Write about your experiences. What was the best part of your experience? Who were you traveling with you or were you solo? How did the trip impact you? What did you learn? What if any challenges?

Date: ______________________________

Location:____________________________

Rate experience:

____

Write about your experiences. What was the best part of your experience? Who were you traveling with you or were you solo? How did the trip impact you? What did you learn? What if any challenges?

____

____

____

____

____

____

____

____

____

____

____

____

____

____

____

Date: ______________________________

Location:____________________________

Rate experience:

____

Write about your experiences. What was the best part of your experience? Who were you traveling with you or were you solo? How did the trip impact you? What did you learn? What if any challenges?

____

____

____

____

____

____

____

____

____

____

____

____

____

____

____

Date: ______________________________

Location:____________________________

Rate experience:

____

Write about your experiences. What was the best part of your experience? Who were you traveling with you or were you solo? How did the trip impact you? What did you learn? What if any challenges?

____

____

____

____

____

____

____

____

____

____

____

____

____

____

____

Date: ______________________________

Location:____________________________

Rate experience:

____

Write about your experiences. What was the best part of your experience? Who were you traveling with you or were you solo? How did the trip impact you? What did you learn? What if any challenges?

____

____

____

____

____

____

____

____

____

____

____

____

____

____

____

Date: ______________________________

Location:____________________________

Rate experience:

____

Write about your experiences. What was the best part of your experience? Who were you traveling with you or were you solo? How did the trip impact you? What did you learn? What if any challenges?

____

____

____

____

____

____

____

____

____

____

____

____

____

____

____

Date: ______________________________

Location:____________________________

Rate experience:

____

Write about your experiences. What was the best part of your experience? Who were you traveling with you or were you solo? How did the trip impact you? What did you learn? What if any challenges?

____

____

____

____

____

____

____

____

____

____

____

____

____

____

____

Date: ______________________________

Location:____________________________

Rate experience:

____

Write about your experiences. What was the best part of your experience? Who were you traveling with you or were you solo? How did the trip impact you? What did you learn? What if any challenges?

____

____

____

____

____

____

____

____

____

____

____

____

____

____

____

Date: ______________________________

Location:____________________________

Rate experience:

____

Write about your experiences. What was the best part of your experience? Who were you traveling with you or were you solo? How did the trip impact you? What did you learn? What if any challenges?

____

____

____

____

____

____

____

____

____

____

____

____

____

____

____

Date: ______________________________

Location:____________________________

Rate experience:

____

Write about your experiences. What was the best part of your experience? Who were you traveling with you or were you solo? How did the trip impact you? What did you learn? What if any challenges?

____

____

____

____

____

____

____

____

____

____

____

____

____

____

____

Date: ______________________________

Location:____________________________

Rate experience:

____

Write about your experiences. What was the best part of your experience? Who were you traveling with you or were you solo? How did the trip impact you? What did you learn? What if any challenges?

____

____

____

____

____

____

____

____

____

____

____

____

____

____

____

Date: ______________________________

Location:____________________________

Rate experience:

____

Write about your experiences. What was the best part of your experience? Who were you traveling with you or were you solo? How did the trip impact you? What did you learn? What if any challenges?

____

____

____

____

____

____

____

____

____

____

____

____

____

____

____

Date: ______________________________

Location:____________________________

Rate experience:

____

Write about your experiences. What was the best part of your experience? Who were you traveling with you or were you solo? How did the trip impact you? What did you learn? What if any challenges?

____

____

____

____

____

____

____

____

____

____

____

____

____

____

____

Date: ______________________________

Location:____________________________

Rate experience:

____

Write about your experiences. What was the best part of your experience? Who were you traveling with you or were you solo? How did the trip impact you? What did you learn? What if any challenges?

____

____

____

____

____

____

____

____

____

____

____

____

____

____

____

Date: ______________________________

Location:____________________________

Rate experience:

____

Write about your experiences. What was the best part of your experience? Who were you traveling with you or were you solo? How did the trip impact you? What did you learn? What if any challenges?

____

____

____

____

____

____

____

____

____

____

____

____

____

____

____

Date: ________________________________

Location:______________________________

Rate experience:

____

Write about your experiences. What was the best part of your experience? Who were you traveling with you or were you solo? How did the trip impact you? What did you learn? What if any challenges?

Date: ______________________________

Location:____________________________

Rate experience:

____

Write about your experiences. What was the best part of your experience? Who were you traveling with you or were you solo? How did the trip impact you? What did you learn? What if any challenges?

____

____

____

____

____

____

____

____

____

____

____

____

____

____

____

Date: ______________________________

Location:____________________________

Rate experience:

____

Write about your experiences. What was the best part of your experience? Who were you traveling with you or were you solo? How did the trip impact you? What did you learn? What if any challenges?

____

____

____

____

____

____

____

____

____

____

____

____

____

____

____

Date: ______________________________

Location:____________________________

Rate experience:

____

Write about your experiences. What was the best part of your experience? Who were you traveling with you or were you solo? How did the trip impact you? What did you learn? What if any challenges?

____

____

____

____

____

____

____

____

____

____

____

____

____

____

____

Date: ______________________________

Location:____________________________

Rate experience:

____

Write about your experiences. What was the best part of your experience? Who were you traveling with you or were you solo? How did the trip impact you? What did you learn? What if any challenges?

____

____

____

____

____

____

____

____

____

____

____

____

____

____

____

Date: ______________________________

Location:____________________________

Rate experience:

____

Write about your experiences. What was the best part of your experience? Who were you traveling with you or were you solo? How did the trip impact you? What did you learn? What if any challenges?

____

____

____

____

____

____

____

____

____

____

____

____

____

____

____

Date: ______________________________

Location:______________________________

Rate experience:

____

Write about your experiences. What was the best part of your experience? Who were you traveling with you or were you solo? How did the trip impact you? What did you learn? What if any challenges?

____

____

____

____

____

____

____

____

____

____

____

____

____

____

____

Date: ______________________________

Location:____________________________

Rate experience:

____

Write about your experiences. What was the best part of your experience? Who were you traveling with you or were you solo? How did the trip impact you? What did you learn? What if any challenges?

____

____

____

____

____

____

____

____

____

____

____

____

____

____

____

Date: ______________________________

Location:____________________________

Rate experience:

____

Write about your experiences. What was the best part of your experience? Who were you traveling with you or were you solo? How did the trip impact you? What did you learn? What if any challenges?

____

____

____

____

____

____

____

____

____

____

____

____

____

____

____

Date: ______________________________

Location:____________________________

Rate experience:

____

Write about your experiences. What was the best part of your experience? Who were you traveling with you or were you solo? How did the trip impact you? What did you learn? What if any challenges?

____

____

____

____

____

____

____

____

____

____

____

____

____

____

____

Date: ______________________________

Location:____________________________

Rate experience:

____

Write about your experiences. What was the best part of your experience? Who were you traveling with you or were you solo? How did the trip impact you? What did you learn? What if any challenges?

____

____

____

____

____

____

____

____

____

____

____

____

____

____

____

Date: ______________________________

Location:____________________________

Rate experience:

____

Write about your experiences. What was the best part of your experience? Who were you traveling with you or were you solo? How did the trip impact you? What did you learn? What if any challenges?

____

____

____

____

____

____

____

____

____

____

____

____

____

____

____

Date: ______________________________

Location:____________________________

Rate experience:

____

Write about your experiences. What was the best part of your experience? Who were you traveling with you or were you solo? How did the trip impact you? What did you learn? What if any challenges?

____

____

____

____

____

____

____

____

____

____

____

____

____

____

____

Date: ______________________________

Location:____________________________

Rate experience:

____

Write about your experiences. What was the best part of your experience? Who were you traveling with you or were you solo? How did the trip impact you? What did you learn? What if any challenges?

Date: ________________________________

Location:______________________________

Rate experience:

____

Write about your experiences. What was the best part of your experience? Who were you traveling with you or were you solo? How did the trip impact you? What did you learn? What if any challenges?

____

____

____

____

____

____

____

____

____

____

____

____

____

____

____

Date: ______________________________

Location:______________________________

Rate experience:

____

Write about your experiences. What was the best part of your experience? Who were you traveling with you or were you solo? How did the trip impact you? What did you learn? What if any challenges?

____

____

____

____

____

____

____

____

____

____

____

____

____

____

____

Date: ______________________________

Location:____________________________

Rate experience:

____

Write about your experiences. What was the best part of your experience? Who were you traveling with you or were you solo? How did the trip impact you? What did you learn? What if any challenges?

____

____

____

____

____

____

____

____

____

____

____

____

____

____

____

Date: ______________________________

Location:____________________________

Rate experience:

____

Write about your experiences. What was the best part of your experience? Who were you traveling with you or were you solo? How did the trip impact you? What did you learn? What if any challenges?

____

____

____

____

____

____

____

____

____

____

____

____

____

____

____

Date: ______________________________

Location:____________________________

Rate experience:

____

Write about your experiences. What was the best part of your experience? Who were you traveling with you or were you solo? How did the trip impact you? What did you learn? What if any challenges?

____

____

____

____

____

____

____

____

____

____

____

____

____

____

____

Date: ______________________________

Location:____________________________

Rate experience:

____

Write about your experiences. What was the best part of your experience? Who were you traveling with you or were you solo? How did the trip impact you? What did you learn? What if any challenges?

____

____

____

____

____

____

____

____

____

____

____

____

____

____

____

Date: ______________________________

Location:____________________________

Rate experience:

____

Write about your experiences. What was the best part of your experience? Who were you traveling with you or were you solo? How did the trip impact you? What did you learn? What if any challenges?

____

____

____

____

____

____

____

____

____

____

____

____

____

____

____

Date: ______________________________

Location:____________________________

Rate experience:

____

Write about your experiences. What was the best part of your experience? Who were you traveling with you or were you solo? How did the trip impact you? What did you learn? What if any challenges?

____

____

____

____

____

____

____

____

____

____

____

____

____

____

____

Date: ______________________________

Location:____________________________

Rate experience:

____

Write about your experiences. What was the best part of your experience? Who were you traveling with you or were you solo? How did the trip impact you? What did you learn? What if any challenges?

____

____

____

____

____

____

____

____

____

____

____

____

____

____

____

Date: ______________________________

Location:____________________________

Rate experience:

____

Write about your experiences. What was the best part of your experience? Who were you traveling with you or were you solo? How did the trip impact you? What did you learn? What if any challenges?

Date: ______________________________

Location:____________________________

Rate experience:

____

Write about your experiences. What was the best part of your experience? Who were you traveling with you or were you solo? How did the trip impact you? What did you learn? What if any challenges?

Date: ______________________________

Location:____________________________

Rate experience:

____

Write about your experiences. What was the best part of your experience? Who were you traveling with you or were you solo? How did the trip impact you? What did you learn? What if any challenges?

____

____

____

____

____

____

____

____

____

____

____

____

____

____

____

Date: ______________________________

Location:____________________________

Rate experience:

____

Write about your experiences. What was the best part of your experience? Who were you traveling with you or were you solo? How did the trip impact you? What did you learn? What if any challenges?

____

____

____

____

____

____

____

____

____

____

____

____

____

____

____

Date: ______________________________

Location:_____________________________

Rate experience:

____

Write about your experiences. What was the best part of your experience? Who were you traveling with you or were you solo? How did the trip impact you? What did you learn? What if any challenges?

Date: ______________________________

Location:____________________________

Rate experience:

____

Write about your experiences. What was the best part of your experience? Who were you traveling with you or were you solo? How did the trip impact you? What did you learn? What if any challenges?

Date: ______________________________

Location:____________________________

Rate experience:

____

Write about your experiences. What was the best part of your experience? Who were you traveling with you or were you solo? How did the trip impact you? What did you learn? What if any challenges?

____

____

____

____

____

____

____

____

____

____

____

____

____

____

____

I WANT TO
VACATION SO
LONG, I FORGET
ALL MY
PASSWORDS.

BUCKET LIST IDEAS

- ☐ Visit every continent.
- ☐ Visit the 7 wonders of the world
- ☐ Trek to Machu Picchu.
- ☐ Go on an African safari.
- ☐ Explore the ancient ruins of Pompeii.
- ☐ Walk the Great Wall of China.
- ☐ Visit the Taj Mahal.
- ☐ Go island hopping in the Greek islands.
- ☐ Explore the beautiful beaches of Bali.
- ☐ Take a road trip through the United States.
- ☐ Visit the ancient pyramids of Egypt.
- ☐ See the cherry blossoms in Japan.
- ☐ Go on a European river cruise.
- ☐ Explore the vibrant city of Rio de Janeiro.
- ☐ See the Northern Lights in Norway.
- ☐ Go snorkeling in the Great Barrier Reef.
- ☐ Take a hot air balloon ride in Cappadocia.
- ☐ Go on a wildlife safari in Tanzania.
- ☐ Go on a luxury train ride through India.
- ☐ Take a cooking class in Italy.
- ☐ Visit the beautiful beaches of Thailand.

- ☐ Go on a trek through the Himalayas.
- ☐ Take a hot air balloon ride in Napa Valley.
- ☐ Visit the beautiful island of Fiji.
- ☐ Go on a camel ride in Dubai
- ☐ Explore the vibrant city of New Orleans.
- ☐ See the cherry blossoms in Washington, D.C.
- ☐ Visit the beautiful city of Vienna.
- ☐ Go on a trek through the Andes.
- ☐ Explore the beautiful city of Barcelona.
- ☐ Visit the beautiful beaches of the Maldives.
- ☐ Explore the ancient city of Athens.
- ☐ Visit the beautiful beaches of Vietnam.
- ☐ Go on a wildlife safari in Botswana.
- ☐ Take a hot air balloon ride in Turkey.
- ☐ Go on a hot air balloon ride in New Zealand.
- ☐ Visit the ancient ruins of Stonehenge in England.
- ☐ Take a surfing lesson in Hawaii.
- ☐ Explore the beautiful city of Prague.
- ☐ Go on a trek through the Amazon rainforest.
- ☐ Take a road trip through Australia.
- ☐ Visit the beautiful city of Amsterdam.

- ☐ Go on a luxury train ride through South Africa.
- ☐ Take a food tour in Japan.
- ☐ Visit the beautiful beaches of Costa Rica.
- ☐ Explore the vibrant city of Marrakech.
- ☐ Go on a European bike tour.
- ☐ Take a hot air balloon ride in South Dakota.
- ☐ Visit the beautiful island of Seychelles.
- ☐ Explore the ancient city of Rome.
- ☐ Go on a luxury train ride through Ireland.
- ☐ Take a cooking class in Spain.
- ☐ Visit the beautiful beaches of Mexico.
- ☐ Explore the vibrant city of Toronto.
- ☐ See the Northern Lights in Finland.
- ☐ Go snorkeling in the Red Sea.
- ☐ Take a hot air balloon ride in Colorado.
- ☐ Visit the beautiful island of Mauritius.
- ☐ Explore the ancient city of Delhi.
- ☐ Go on a luxury train ride through Wales.
- ☐ Take a cooking class in Morocco.
- ☐ Visit the beautiful beaches of Indonesia.
- ☐ Explore the vibrant city of Berlin.
- ☐ Go on a European hiking tour.
- ☐ Take a hot air balloon ride in California.

☐ Go on a wildlife safari in South Africa.
☐ Visit the beautiful island of Bora Bora.
☐ Go on a luxury train ride through Austria.
☐ Take a cooking class in Thailand.
☐ Visit the beautiful beaches of the Philippines.
☐ Go snorkeling in the Mediterranean Sea.
☐ Take a hot air balloon ride in Texas.
☐ Visit the beautiful monkey forest of Bali.
☐ Take a cooking class in Portugal.
☐ Go on a luxury train ride through Switzerland.
☐ Explore the vibrant city of Singapore.
☐ See the Northern Lights in Canada.
☐ Go snorkeling in the Pacific Ocean.
☐ Take a hot air balloon ride in New Mexico.
☐ Go on a wildlife safari in Madagascar.
☐ Visit the beautiful island of Tahiti.
☐ Explore the ancient city of Petra.
☐ Go on a luxury train ride through the Netherlands.
☐ Take a cooking class in India.
☐ Explore the vibrant city of Istanbul.
☐ Go on a European art tour.
☐ Take a hot air balloon ride in Utah.
☐ Visit the beautiful island of Hawaii.

- ☐ Go on a luxury train ride through Austria.
- ☐ Take a cooking class in Thailand.
- ☐ Go snorkeling in the Mediterranean Sea.
- ☐ Visit the beautiful island of Bali.
- ☐ Go on a luxury train ride through Germany.
- ☐ Take a cooking class in Portugal.
- ☐ Explore the vibrant city of Montreal.
- ☐ See the cherry blossoms in China.
- ☐ Go on a wildlife safari in Rwanda.
- ☐ Visit the beautiful island of Santorini.
- ☐ Explore the ancient city of Cairo.
- ☐ Go on a luxury train ride through Switzerland.
- ☐ Visit the beautiful beaches of the Bahamas.
- ☐ Take a Spanish class in Mexico
- ☐ Explore the vibrant city of Tokyo.
- ☐ See the Northern Lights in Denmark.
- ☐ Go snorkeling in the Indian Ocean.
- ☐ Take a hot air balloon ride in Oregon.
- ☐ Go on a wildlife safari in the Serengeti.
- ☐ Visit the beautiful island of the Galapagos.
- ☐ Explore the ancient city of Persepolis.
- ☐ Go on a luxury train ride through Spain.
- ☐ Take a cooking class in China.

- ☐ Visit the beautiful beaches of Puerto Rico.
- ☐ Explore the vibrant city of Cape Town.
- ☐ Go on a European history tour.
- ☐ Take a hot air balloon ride in Vermont.
- ☐ Safari in Tanzania.
- ☐ Visit the beautiful island of Tahiti.
- ☐ Explore the ancient city of Petra.
- ☐ Go on a luxury train ride through the Netherlands.
- ☐ Take a cooking class in India.
- ☐ Go snorkeling in the Mediterranean Sea.
- ☐ Visit the beautiful island of Bali.
- ☐ Explore the ancient city of Jerusalem.
- ☐ Take a cooking class in Portugal.
- ☐ Visit the beautiful beaches of the Dominican Republic.
- ☐ Go on a trek through the Grand Canyon.
- ☐ Go on a European city tour.
- ☐ Safari in Rwanda.
- ☐ Explore the ancient city of Cairo.
- ☐ Go on a luxury train ride through Switzerland.
- ☐ Take a cooking class in Brazil.
- ☐ Explore the vibrant city of Sydney.
- ☐ See the Northern Lights in Iceland.
- ☐ Go white water rafting on the Colorado River.
- ☐ Take a skydiving lesson.
- ☐ Go on a whale watching tour.

- ☐ Go on a camel Safari in the Sahara desert.
- ☐ Take a scuba diving lesson and explore the world beneath the waves.
- ☐ Go bungee jumping off a bridge or cliff.
- ☐ Take a hot air balloon ride over the Loire Valley in France.
- ☐ Go on a horseback riding tour through the Patagonia region of Argentina.
- ☐ Take a sailing trip through the Mediterranean Sea.
- ☐ Go on a trek to the base camp of Mount Everest.
- ☐ Take a paragliding lesson and soar above the mountains.
- ☐ Go on a fishing expedition in the Amazon rainforest.
- ☐ Take a snowboarding lesson in the Swiss Alps.
- ☐ Go on a safari through the Okavango Delta in Botswana.
- ☐ Go on a kayaking trip through the Grand Canyon.
- ☐ Take a skydiving lesson over the Great Barrier Reef.
- ☐ Take a hot air balloon ride over the vineyards of Bordeaux, France.
- ☐ Go on a trek to the base camp of Mount Kilimanjaro.
- ☐ Take a paragliding lesson and soar above the beaches of Costa Rica.

- ☐ Go on a fishing expedition in the Gulf of Mexico.
- ☐ Go on a Safari through the Masai Mara National Reserve in Kenya.
- ☐ Take a snowshoeing tour through the Adirondacks.
- ☐ Take a skydiving lesson over the beaches of Hawaii.
- ☐ Go on a horseback riding tour through the Swiss Alps.
- ☐ Take a hot air balloon ride over the rolling hills of Tuscany, Italy.
- ☐ Go on a trek to the base camp of Mount Fuji.
- ☐ Take a paragliding lesson and soar above the beaches of the Caribbean.
- ☐ Go on a fishing expedition in the Pacific Northwest.
- ☐ Take a snowboarding lesson in the Italian Dolomites.
- ☐ Go on a safari through the Serengeti National Park in Tanzania.
- ☐ Take a skydiving lesson over the beaches of Thailand.
- ☐ Take a hot air balloon ride over the vineyards of Napa Valley, California.
- ☐ Go on a trek to the base camp of Mount Rainier.
- ☐ Take a paragliding lesson and soar above the beaches of Bali.
- ☐ Glacier Bay in Alaska.
- ☐ Take a snowboarding

lesson in the Austrian Alps.

- ☐ Go on a kayaking trip through the Grand Canyon.
- ☐ Take a skydiving lesson over the beaches of Australia.
- ☐ Take a yoga retreat in Bali.
- ☐ Go on a meditation retreat in Thailand.
- ☐ Take a spa vacation in Japan.
- ☐ Go on a wellness retreat in Costa Rica.
- ☐ Go to Antarctica to see polar bears
- ☐ Go on a wellness retreat in Mexico.
- ☐ Go on a meditation retreat in Indonesia.
- ☐ Take a spa vacation in Italy.
- ☐ Go to Carnival in Brazil.
- ☐ Go on a meditation retreat in the Philippines.
- ☐ Take a spa vacation in Turkey.
- ☐ Go on a wellness retreat in Peru.
- ☐ Take a yoga retreat in Spain.
- ☐ Go to the markets in Morocco.
- ☐ Take a history tour in Germany.
- ☐ Go on a wellness retreat in Chile.
- ☐ Take a yoga retreat in Portugal.
- ☐ Go on a meditation retreat in Bali.
- ☐ Take a spa vacation in France.
- ☐ Stay in a luxury villa in the Maldives.
- ☐ Stay in a luxury castle in Scotland.
- ☐ Go on a luxury yacht charter in

the Mediterranean.

- ☐ Stay in a luxury villa in Bali.
- ☐ Go on a luxury safari in Tanzania.
- ☐ Stay in a luxury castle in Ireland.
- ☐ Go on a luxury yacht charter in the Caribbean.
- ☐ Stay in a luxury villa in Thailand.
- ☐ Go on a luxury safari in Kenya.
- ☐ Stay in a luxury castle in Wales.
- ☐ Go on a luxury yacht charter in the Greek islands.
- ☐ Stay in a luxury villa in the Seychelles.
- ☐ Go on a luxury safari in Botswana.
- ☐ Stay in a luxury castle in France.
- ☐ Go on a luxury yacht charter in the Aegean Sea.
- ☐ Stay in a luxury villa in Italy.
- ☐ Go on a luxury safari in Zambia.
- ☐ Stay in a luxury castle in Germany.
- ☐ Go on a luxury yacht charter in the Adriatic Sea.
- ☐ Stay in a luxury villa in the Bahamas.
- ☐ Stay in a luxury castle in the Czech Republic.
- ☐ Stay in a luxury villa in Portugal.
- ☐ Go on a luxury yacht charter in the Ionian Sea.

BUCKET LIST

- [ ]
- [ ]
- [ ]
- [ ]
- [ ]
- [ ]
- [ ]
- [ ]
- [ ]
- [ ]
- [ ]
- [ ]
- [ ]
- [ ]
- [ ]
- [ ]
- [ ]
- [ ]
- [ ]
- [ ]
- [ ]
- [ ]
- [ ]
- [ ]

- [ ] ______
- [ ] ______
- [ ] ______
- [ ] ______
- [ ] ______
- [ ] ______
- [ ] ______
- [ ] ______
- [ ] ______
- [ ] ______
- [ ] ______
- [ ] ______
- [ ] ______
- [ ] ______
- [ ] ______
- [ ] ______
- [ ] ______
- [ ] ______
- [ ] ______
- [ ] ______
- [ ] ______
- [ ] ______
- [ ] ______
- [ ] ______

☐ ___
☐ ___
☐ ___
☐ ___
☐ ___
☐ ___
☐ ___
☐ ___
☐ ___
☐ ___
☐ ___
☐ ___
☐ ___
☐ ___
☐ ___
☐ ___
☐ ___
☐ ___
☐ ___
☐ ___
☐ ___
☐ ___
☐ ___
☐ ___

DISCLAIMER: *There are many quotes included in the list that are attributed to "unknown" authors because the original source of the quote could not be determined. It is common for quotes to be shared and passed down through the years, and often the original source is lost or forgotten. In many cases, these quotes have been widely circulated and attributed to "unknown" or "anonymous" rather than a specific individual.*

It is important to note that these quotes are included for their value as thought-provoking prompts and inspiration, and not as a means to attribute credit to a specific individual.

Made in the USA
Middletown, DE
24 February 2023

25435455R00110